Minimalist Living:

Declutter Your Home, Schedule & Digital Life for Simple Living (and Discover that Less is More)

2nd Edition: Updated & Expanded

ASTON SANDERSON

"Minimalist Living" by Aston Sanderson. Published by Walnut Publishing Company, Hanover Park, IL 60133

www.walnutpub.com

© 2017 Walnut Publishing.

BONUS: BOOK CLUB INVITE

Before we get started with this Minimalist Living book, we wanted to tell you how much we appreciate you as a reader, and that we want to invite you to our Free Book Club.

When you subscribe, you get first access to discounted and free new releases from or small publishing house, Walnut Publishing.

Claim your invite at www.walnutpub.com.

Thanks for buying, and enjoy reading.

Note from the Author

Thank you for purchasing "Minimalist Living: Declutter Your Home, Schedule & Digital Life for Simple Living (and Discover that Less is More)."

I hope you will learn a lot of valuable information that you can apply to your own life, as well as have some fun and be entertained!

I worked hard to write this book with you, my reader, in mind. Whether you enjoyed the book, or you think I got some things wrong, I'd love to hear from you.

I personally read all my reviews on Amazon, and love to hear from my readers. If you can take a minute to just write at least one line about what you thought of my book, I'd be really grateful.

Type this URL into your browser to go straight to the review page for this book: INSERTLINK

I really appreciate it, and now, let's get to the book!

—Aston Sanderson

TABLE OF CONTENTS

1 INTRODUCTION

WELCOME TO "MINIMALIST LIVING." THE basic principle of this book is: You have too much stuff. And it's not making you happy. In fact, I'd wager that all your extra stuff is making you decidedly unhappy.

But there's a way out from underneath that pile of stuff that's weighing you down and holding you back.

We'll discuss the underlying reasons that you, me, your friends, your coworkers, strangers on the street — all of us — are so compelled to buy, and why we clutter our lives in the first place.

We'll use economics and philosophy principles to look at consumerism and minimalism.

We'll discuss your custom minimalism plan, and why a minimalist lifestyle doesn't match what you've probably seen it portrayed as in the media: It doesn't mean living with bare, white walls, one lamp, one chair and owning just two outfits.

You'll learn how to win back your sanity, time, money and freedom to live a life that is not minimal, but that is abundant in your values and what matters to you.

We will save your life from your stuff.

Are you ready?

2 WHAT IS MINIMALISM?

TO UNDERSTAND MINIMALISM, I'M GOING to ask you to start with a simple question. The question is:

Have you ever packed for a vacation or trip?

If your answer is yes, then you have already practiced minimalism.

Minimalism can feel very inaccessible and unreasonable to those who have only heard about it from news articles. You've probably wondered if minimalism is really for you, if you have the strength to narrow down your possessions, or if you would be the same person without all your things. These questions are normal, and a misunderstanding of what minimalism can be has made it seem inaccessible to many people. But there's a reason minimalism was brought on your radar, and a reason you are reading this book right now. You want to see if it is for you.

And as we learned with my vacation packing question, you have already tried minimalism. And guess what? You're still alive!

Minimalism is *en vogue* at the moment, and that means that every decluttering guru, minimalist blogger and minimalist author (who convinces you to get rid of all your things but at the same time, buy their book for your coffee table) has a guaranteed method to make you finally happy. You can be just like the extreme minimalism guru once you follow their plan. Once you get rid of all of your clothes, your home and your devices, you too can live in a van, own three shirts, two pairs of pants and one pair of shoes, and grow your own vegetables out on the open plains.

OK, maybe I am exaggerating a bit. But many minimalists live in barren, cold apartments with barely any possessions. They say this makes them truly happy.

But my form of minimalism is different. My minimalism is for everyone, not just extremists. And I am going to do something very radical with my minimalism book: I am not going to promise I can make you happy.

Crazy, right?

But you have come to the point where you are looking at minimalism as a lifestyle because you've acquired an overwhelming amount of stuff and you've realized that it doesn't make you happy. Things aren't going to make you happy. But guess what? The *absence* of things isn't going to make you happy either.

So, if you follow the advice in this book, what can it give you? Paring down your possessions — we'll talk home, clothes, schedule and time commitments, digital clutter and more — gives you the space and room, free from distraction, to explore what does make you happy. I can't promise you happiness, but I can promise that you're taking the first step toward it by making the space for happiness in your life.

When you pare down what isn't essential in your life, you make the room to discover what is essential. Often, what is essential and happiness-making is doing fulfilling work, investing in meaningful relationships with the people in our lives, and focusing on improving our physical and mental health over improving our "status" as displayed by our possessions, apartment and flashy car.

But we'll talk about that more in future chapters. For now, let's get back to that travel metaphor.

No matter whether you are a light packer or a heavy-duty packer who prepares for every possibility, just by packing for a vacation, you have practiced paring down your things. So even if you packed three large suitcases for a weekend beach getaway, you still practiced whittling down your possessions from a house- or apartment-full to just three suitcases. How did you decide what was essential? If you were going to a warm, beach climate, you probable brought at least a swimsuit, suntan lotion, and a good book. You probably left at home your fall jacket, your desktop computer, and the other 100 books on your book shelf.

You spent a week by the shore, and you didn't need all those things you left at home. In fact, many people, when their luggage gets lost on their holiday, find that they enjoy their vacation more once they buy some random clothes and accept that they just can't have the things they intended to bring. You will find that embracing minimalism can feel freeing in the same way. At first, getting rid of things and adapting to a new philosophy and way of life will be uncomfortable and scary, and you may feel compelled to turn back. But once you relax, open yourself up to the experience, and allow the benefits of minimalism into your life, you will be pleasantly surprised.

Now that you've had a brief introduction to this renegade style of minimalism, and have breathed a sigh of relief that I'm not going to try to convince you to live in a small, barren and white apartment, we can begin to start diving deeper into the psychology of consumerism and minimalism.

In the next chapter, we'll examine the different reasons we humans love to collect so much stuff in the first place.

3 WHY WE CLUTTER OUR LIVES

PEOPLE COLLECT POSSESSIONS AND KNICK knacks for so many reasons. In this chapter, we'll look at a few reasons that we get so buried in our lives under all that clutter and stuff.

The first reason that people buy excessively is that they are trying to fill a void. I know I have experienced this, and I'm sure you have, too. That void may be many things: Perhaps it is a particularly hurtful breakup in a relationship, perhaps it is the loss of a relative, perhaps the loss of a job, a dissatisfaction with work, or any other feeling of inadequacy or lack. When someone tries to fill a void with shopping, they can never patch the hurt, not permanently. A person will try to distract themselves from feelings of worthlessness or grief by putting a temporary patch of retail therapy over the wound. But the rush that shopping provides does not last or sustain us in any meaningful way.

The dopamine rush of purchasing something new actually ends the second we buy the item (or shortly after unboxing it, if you enjoy unboxing). Psychology shows that people actually get more of a dopamine rush (the chemicals that create feelings of pleasure in our brains) from anticipating a purchase than actually making it. Once you buy something, it becomes just another old thing you own that you are unhappy with. It may not happen right away, but I bet it happens more quickly than you think that the things you own become dusty, gray, old and boring in your eyes. Think about it: Everything you own now was once a new item to you. Some things may have been hand-me-downs, but many things you own were probably purchased new. You probably anticipated buying the item before you went to the store, maybe you spent hours or days researching online the different options available to you, you agonized over making the right purchase, and then you felt excited on purchase day. Handing over your hard-earned money for the item was satisfying, but once you got it, you were a bit disappointed to see you weren't significantly happier than before you owned the item, at least on a consistent daily basis. And now, you barely think about that item or your much-anticipated purchase. You may even be thinking about upgrading to a different model, different color, better quality, or just newer version. What was once so craved by you now leaves a bad taste in your mouth. And so the rapid consumption cycle goes.

So if you are shopping and acquiring things to fill a void within yourself, you need to recognize this feeling. We'll talk more about dealing with this feeling later, but first, let's identify another reason you may be shopping and buying things.

Another reason that we as humans buy excessively, as opposed to filling a void, is to attain an ideal. This is called aspirational living. Basically, it's the idea of trying to live your life like an Instagram celebrity or a model in a magazine. You want to buy a lamp or end table to "finally complete the look of the living room," or buy a pair of earrings or a new dress to have "the perfect thing to wear for the weekend party." But it's hard to actually attain these goals: The Instagram pictures are filtered and photoshopped, the homes in the magazines don't exist and no one lives in them.

Let's look at two ways aspirational living hurts us. When we look for perfection outside ourselves, we can never fully grasp it. If you try to satisfy a feeling you have inside of you by having a nice living room, or a great outfit, that thing is not you. It's another thing you own. It exists outside of you. You can only find true happiness from within yourself. Another way this assumption about attaining perfection is harmful is that perfection is never an attainable goal, or at least it isn't one that leaves us satisfied. Perfection is hard to maintain. Those who strive for it in any area of life will find themselves struggling to be happy with anything, even something that is 95% "perfect." They can only look at how something lacks, or what it is missing, instead of appreciating what is. There are so many wonderful things in life, but a perfectionist can only focus on what's missing from the picture. Living your life this way is a guarantee to live unhappily.

Those are the two main reasons we acquire stuff: We either want to stave off feelings of lack, or we crave a feeling of fullness. No matter which end of the spectrum drives us, neither are healthy reasons to spend the money you work your whole life to earn just to acquire things you have to take care of.

In the next chapter, we will look at how you can stop living a life driven by these feelings, and how you can live a life of abundance, and what that means.

4 Living a Life of Abundance

Minimalism may sound like the opposite of abundance. Abundance means a very large quantity of something. So you could say most people are already living lives of abundance: They have so many possessions cluttering up their lives, they are basically swimming in abundance! But in this chapter, we are going to explore a new definition of abundance.

People often think that minimalism means living with almost no possessions in a barren home. But minimalism is just a sliding scale and spectrum, and an optional path to happiness. Maybe you want to reject the idea of minimalism. If you do, that is your choice. But first, ask yourself: Are you possessions, and your goals to acquire more and nicer possessions with each passing year, really making you happy? If not, it's imperative that you re-assess your relationship to the things you own. This is all minimalism is inviting you to do. You can decide how many of your possessions you want to keep, which of them to keep, and why. I will not direct you to get rid of all of your spatulas, DVDs, or old high school year books. As long as you take the basics of minimalism as you learn them here, and use them to re-assess your priorities, and you live by your priorities, then you have succeeded in minimalism.

So living a life of abundance doesn't mean owning many things; what it actually means is living a life that is abundant in the areas that are important to you.

The hard part is figuring out what is important to you. And then once you've figured that out, you must invest in those areas. The ideas in this book aren't easy, and they aren't quick-fixes. But they are changes that are possible to make, and the results you see can be incredible.

So, on to the hard questions: What are some areas you can choose to invest in, some aspects of your life in which you'd like to experience abundance? For many people, family is important. Another area that many people find important is meaningful work that contributes to society. While some people pursue this at their 9-to-5 job that they get paid for, others pursue meaningful work by volunteering or by investing in an artistic passion. Another area some people find great to invest in is their own physical body and health. People accomplish this by spending time being active by going on hikes, playing a team sport, or going to the gym while nourishing their body with healthy food and regular sleep.

While these are just general examples, refocusing your energy, time and money into these areas of your life can have so many lasting benefits that far outweigh the short, addictive highs of shopping and acquiring. Establishing meaningful relationships with friends or family is a basic human need, and has long-lasting effects on our mental and physical health. Being a part of a community is important. Pursuing meaningful work makes us feel needed on this Earth, and like we have bettered the world around us. Taking care of our body leads to better mental fitness as well. Exercising releases endorphins, and being of sound physical mind and body means calmer, healthier approach to every aspect of our life. Physical health is often referred to as a "cornerstone" habit. Once you put more exercise or a better diet into your life, you will start to find that it leads to the formation of other healthy habits and benefits in all areas of life.

OK, are you asking yourself: Why all this blathering on about family, work and health? Isn't this a book about minimalism? You caught me! But the point of this chapter is to convince you that minimalism doesn't mean throwing away, getting rid, reducing, and cutting out until there is almost nothing left in your life.

Minimalism is cutting away the inessential, to make more room for the essential.

Minimalism is about minimal waste of time, energy, resources and money and maximum gain from time, energy, resources and money. Minimalists strive to live lives of abundance. It's just that usually, the abundance they collect and invest in isn't something you can see. It isn't a perfectly hip and well-decorated apartment, or the most chic wardrobe.

Instead, it is investment in intangibles, but the things that are most likely to bring us true and lasting happiness.

Now that you understand what we're going for with living a life of abundance, in the next chapter, we'll talk about the 80/20 rule, another guiding principle of minimalism that may be new to you.

5 THE 80/20 RULE

THE 80/20 RULE (ALSO known as the 80/20 Principle or the Pareto Principle) is the general idea that 80% of the effects of something come from just 20% of the causes. The rule can be a bit hard to grasp at first, but once you get it, it can change your life.

The principle was developed by an Italian economist, Vilifredo Pareto, who first published his principle in a paper in 1896. He noticed the principle in many areas of his life, from big to small. He noticed that 80% of the land in Italy was owned by roughly 20% of the Italian population. He also noticed that in his backyard garden, 20% of the pea pods produced 80% of the peas. From a huge swath of land as big as a country, to the smallest pea in a garden, Pareto realized that the 80/20 rule was everywhere around us.

The 80/20 rule will apply to your life in small and huge ways, as well. The principle is often referenced in business circles. For instance, 80% of sales usually come from 20% of customers. In addition, 80% of complaints usually come from 20% of customers (and the most difficult-to-please customers are usually not the same customers who are producing 80% of the income).

How does this economics law relate to minimalism?

The applications of this rule are never-ending. Once you start looking for areas where the 80/20 rule applies, you will see them everywhere. You are probably using 20% of your kitchen utensils 80% of the time. You are probably wearing 20% of your clothes 80% of the time. You are probably accomplishing 80% of your best work (whether it's at your job, tidying your home, catching up on emails, etc.) in 20% of your time.

Following the Pareto Principle, you could probably pare down about 80% of your possessions and time-wasting and have that much more time and money to devote to intentional living, or living a life of abundance.

In terms of time, instead of spending five hours trying to complete a work task, and bouncing around between Facebook, emails, Instagram, reading four different articles, talking to your coworker, going to the bathroom, going to grab a snack, writing your grocery list and checking Facebook again, you could probably laser-focus your attention on your task, forcing yourself to complete it in 30-minute chunks, in less than two hours. We'll bring in another economics law here to explain this. Have you heard of Parkinson's Law? Parkinson's Law states, "Work expands so as to fill the time available for its completion." Often, we are trying to waste time at work because we have to clock in from 9 to 5. But if you kept track of how long each of your tasks take, you may find that there is much room for minimizing the time you spend on tasks.

While minimalism is often thought of as re-organizing your closet, it is a philosophy that can be applied to any area of life, especially with managing your time. If you are trying to create more abundance in your life by paring down your possessions, you won't feel like your life is very different if you're still spending 2 hours a day on Facebook and 4 hours in front of Netflix. So when you go through paring down your possessions, your schedule and your digital devices, remember the 80/20 rule. What are you getting the most from? What are you getting little, if anything from? Keep only the 20% that gives you 80% of the results.

Though I mentioned that most people think minimalism is just re-organizing your closet, going through your possessions is still a very important part of the philosophy. (I know you wanted to get out of cleaning out your closet, or basement, or attic, or wherever it is that gives you a headache just thinking about it. But don't worry, I'll guide you through it in later chapters). For now, we'll move onto the next chapter, where we will discuss how living a life of minimalism will save you time and money.

6 How to Save Time & Money

Minimalism can save you both time and money when it comes to possessions.

American society is a consumption-driven culture. Everyone is out to sell you something, and if someone promises that they aren't selling you something, they're lying to you. That's a common saying and a quite cynical view of modern society, but the U.S. is a world power because of its powerful consumption and capitalism.

A well-thought-out critique of global political and economics systems is beyond the scope of this book (and the background of this author), but suffice it to say that if you live in America (or many other developed nations in the world), you probably own too much stuff.

Have you ever thought about the booming self-storage industry, begetting entertaining but horrifying shows like "Storage Wars?" While storage is a necessity in life for people moving houses, going traveling for an extended period of time, or helping family downsize or relocate, self-storage is often not temporary for Americans. We don't only use storage when we're in-between life stages, we use it as a permanent solution to the stuff falling out of our closets and taking over the den.

We have to move into bigger apartments, buy bigger houses, or buy even more complicated storage methods for our closets and pantries to use every available inch of space, from floor to ceiling.

Getting rid of some of this stuff clogging up your life can make you feel like a huge weight has been lifted off your shoulders. Taking care of our things takes up a lot of our time, and can deplete our bank accounts as well, when we have to pay for maintenance, storage, cleaning, care and repair. If you've ever moved from one apartment to another, or even worse, from one house to another, you know the overwhelming feeling of, "How did I ever acquire all this stuff?" When we move, all of our possession are pulled out in front of us, and we can finally see all that we own. Sometimes the result can be quite shocking.

So we have to enlist friends, or hire movers, or rent a truck, just to cart our things from one place to another. If you only pared down to the essentials, you would be confident that any resources you spent moving them from one location to another, storing them, or otherwise spending extra time and money on them was a good investment, because they were things you used often, cared about, and enjoyed. But too many of our possessions are things we don't care about, things we rarely if ever use, and items that we don't actually need or want.

Not buying all these objects in the first place is, of course, the best way to save money. But we'll address that in the next chapter. We'll also address how to go through your items methodically to decide what you would like to keep later on. But for now, let's look at how getting rid of the things you already own can save you money.

The first way to make money from your things is to sell them second-hand. While some of your possessions are used, they may be in quite good working order. Electronics can often sell well on the second-hand market, as well as quality clothing. But you may find, like many people, that many of the things you have are not even opened or ever used! A quick way to make some cash from your old things that you don't want anymore is to hold a garage sale or yard sale. Even if you only make a few bucks off of each person who stops by to browse, the money adds up over several days and across many possessions.

If you find yourself something of an entrepreneur, you can also take to the online second-hand market. You can resell used items on eBay and Amazon, though some effort must be put into creating the descriptions, taking and uploading attractive photos, and then shipping your item to whoever purchases it. Once you learn the ropes of these sites, however, they are surprisingly simple and easy to sell on, and a great way to make a small side income from things you are already own that are just gathering dust around the house. Even putting in a few hours a week can produce quite a bit of extra cash, and it can be fun to watch the auction bidding.

Another way to sell your items is to go to your local thrift store or pawn shop. While many second-hand stores also take donations, some will purchase high-quality items.

The last way to make money is to donate all the things you don't want to your local charity, Good Will or Salvation Army-type store. While the donation is free, you will get a receipt from your donation and can deduct the perceived worth of your items from your next year's taxes. But be aware that how much you think your items are worth is usually much higher than their actual value! So estimate low amounts on your taxes as a safe bet.

So, now you understand how having fewer possessions will save you time in the care for them, and save (or maybe even make!) you money when you get rid of them. In the next chapter, we will look at the toughest part of minimalism: How to want what you already have.

7 How to Want What You Already Have

One of the hardest things in minimalism is truly wanting what you already have.

Feelings of contentment go against human nature by its very design. Intrinsically, in our very basic needs, we always crave what we don't have. It is like the saying, "The grass is always greener on the other side." If you can't decide between two shirts, and you buy the blue one, the gray one is sure to seem better in hindsight. But if you buy the gray one, the blue one suddenly seems the better choice. While this is an over-simplified example, I bet you can think of five items off the top of your head at this moment that you'd like to have or are considering purchasing soon.

Advertising and media can have a lot of influence over us. Actors and actresses in movies are beautiful and skinny, women in makeup commercials have flawless skin and professional athletes have perfectly sculpted bodies. Perfection seems to be all around us, constantly. If only we could look better, have nicer things, or not make mistakes, we, too, could be perfectly happy, and desire nothing else in our lives.

When we look at a beauty product, electronic gadget or new item that we crave, we envision ourselves living in the fantasy world created by advertising. Every area of our life would improve. If we lose 10 pounds, we will no longer get angry in a traffic jam. If we have the new iPhone, we'll suddenly also acquire the perfect romantic partner to take Instagram pictures with. If we have a flashy car, we'll be the type of person who vacations in the Greek isles.

We all get lost in these daydreams to some extent. Maybe you don't identify with believing your entire life will change because of acquiring a possession, but there's a deep-seated, emotional need for you craving it. Why else do you want a new dress, or a new shirt, or a new hat or pair of shoes? Unless you literally don't have any other shoes to wear, or clothes to adorn your body, you crave this thing because of some material reason. Many people all over the world own much less than the average American. They may only have two outfits and one pair of shoes, and yet, they survive. So packing our closets full (and feeling like we have "nothing to wear" when we look at dozens of outfits in our closet) is an irrational need. These irrational needs are making us unhappy.

I ask you to take a few minutes to truly think about and question your thought patterns when you decide that you need the latest tech device or new clothes or accessories. Do you really "need" it, or do you just "want" it? Unless you look deeper within yourself for the reason you are buying things, no amount of decluttering of your home will stop you from filling it back up. You need to look at the true root cause of your consumerism. Maybe you impulsively buy because you are putting off a big creative project, like writing a book, starting a blog, or getting back into painting. Maybe you are dissatisfied with the way you look, but instead of addressing the health of the body under the clothes, you keep purchasing new clothes, thinking you'll finally find the outfit that makes you feel good in your skin. Maybe you are worried or unfulfilled in a relationship in your life, and you buy to fill that need. Whatever the reason is for filling your life with more things, you need to take stock of it.

Figuring out just why you are buying things is the first step to stopping the flow of new things coming into your life. But the second step is actually appreciating the things you already have. How can you do this?

Negative Visualization

One method, as borrowed from the ancient philosophy of stoicism, is called "negative visualization." What negative visualization means is that you imagine losing the things you have, and what your life would be like without them. Sure, your raincoat feels a bit worn, as you've had it for a few years, and you'd really love to get an expensive, new and stylish rain coat. But let's imagine that you no longer want to buy the new one, because you've identified the real reason you are using retail therapy. So now you are just left a bit unhappy with your current coat. But with negative visualization, you imagine losing that coat. What if you have to leave the house, and now you have no rain coat? You suddenly appreciate how it kept you dry, how it was so easy to grab on your way out the door, how it never let you down in four years of owning it. Now when you step outside in the rain, you'll feel more appreciative of your raincoat.

You can use negative visualization for anything in your life. Maybe you have an old phone, and would really like the latest model. But imagine you had no phone at all. How would you find map directions on-the-go, or message friends and loved ones, or take photos of good times to remember them? The capabilities of your phone, even if it is a few years old, are enormous and amazing compared to technology 30 years ago. Taking a minute to think about how amazing this technology is can make you feel a bit more appreciative of the electronics you have, and how they make your life easier.

To create fulfillment in your life, you have to live in the now, and appreciate your life as it is. You can't keep thinking about how great your life will be when you get married, get a promotion, have a bigger apartment, finally live alone, finish writing that book, or lose 10 pounds. Working toward goals is admirable, but you can't sit around waiting to achieve your goals to start loving, appreciating and enjoying your life — that has to start today. And it starts with enjoying what you have in your life at this very moment.

Mindfulness

Like negative visualization, another technique to appreciate what you have is mindfulness. Mindfulness is often confused with meditation in today's society, but the two are extremely similar. Mindfulness is usually seen as a kind of "living" meditation, meaning you can practice it anywhere. You can practice it at your desk at work, while going for a walk, while doing the dishes, or reading a book. You can practice mindfulness anytime, anywhere, and no one needs to know you are doing it.

To practice mindfulness, focus on your five senses: Touch, Smell, Sight, Sound and Taste. Ask yourself what each of these senses is experiencing. What does the keyboard feel like under your fingers at work? Can you hear dogs barking, birds chirping or the wind through the leaves on your walk? Can you see the words on the page as you read a book? What does the dish soap smell like? Even if you are not eating, ask yourself if you can taste anything in your mouth. If not, that's perfectly OK. Even if the answer is "nothing," you are still practicing being aware of your senses.

If you are experienced in practicing mindfulness, you can also observe the rhythm of your breath, your thoughts, and the way your physical body feels during this exercise.

When you practice mindfulness, you have to be in the present moment as you ask yourself these questions. You are concentrating on the here and now. Being more present in the moment has been shown to make people happier. Even if your present situation is not ideal, being present in it is allowing it to just be. When you practice mindfulness, you become more aware of your surroundings, and more in tune with what you have and experience now, instead of living in your thoughts of the past or future. In this way, you will come to appreciate more of what you already have.

Gratitude

The last technique we will use for wanting what we already have is gratitude. Studies show that writing down things we are thankful for just once a day has a huge improvement on our mood and happiness overall. To practice gratitude, you can write a list of three things you are grateful for when you wake up in the morning, or before you got to bed at night. You can choose three separate things, or just one thing and write three reasons you are grateful for it. At first, it may be hard to think of things you are grateful for. But once you start to practice this, you will find that you can be grateful for nearly anything and everything. For example, you may start with a list like this:

I am grateful for my loving spouse
I am grateful to have a job
I am grateful for my health

And eventually end up thinking up creative things to be grateful for, like this:

I am grateful for my feet, and that I can walk from place to place

I am grateful for the stars, and that I get to look at them at night
I am grateful for salt, because it enhances the taste of my meals

It doesn't matter what you write down, as long as you spend a few minutes appreciating what you have to be grateful for in life.

To summarize, the three ways to want what you already have are to practice negative visualization, mindfulness and gratitude. In the first place, though, you have to investigate what feelings are causing you to keep buying, and address those. In the next chapter, we will look at how being frugal — spending less and buying less — can actually be more fun than buying.

8 FRUGALITY CAN BE FUN

REMEMBER THE THOUGHT EXPERIMENT FROM the first chapter of this book, in which I asked you if you had ever packed for a vacation? To illustrate a little bit of fun frugality to start off this chapter, let's revisit that question.

So, imagine you packed for your beach vacation, and now you've arrived at your destination. But let's say you forgot to bring those essentials: your swimsuit, suntan lotion, and a good book. If you're going to a vacation destination, chances are you could easily buy all three. There are probably shops at the airport you land in that have all three, in fact. You might pay a bit more, but your trip hasn't been ruined. Or, you could probably find a department store that has all three in the city you are visiting. If you are on a remote island, you can still find small shops or your hotel gift shop that will have (if even a small selection) swim suits and sunscreen. Can't find a bookstore? You can download the Kindle app on your phone and buy electronically, borrow a book from another guest or someone you meet on your holiday, or decide to spend vacation writing instead of reading.

In our example, forgetting these essential items was probably a bit of an annoyance, but you figured out how to acquire them. It just took some patience, some creativity, and a bit of luck. Perhaps when you borrowed a book from a fellow traveler, you met someone new and made a lasting connection. Perhaps your garish gift shop swimsuit caused the taxi driver to remember you, and he gives you a discount on your rides the rest of the trip. Perhaps when you forgot your 15 SPF suntan lotion, you had to buy 50 SPF at the store instead. But the sun's heat was intense, and you would had been severely burned and ruined your trip without the higher SPF.

Things will always go wrong in some way. When you are able to ride these mishaps out, you may find that the surprises they have in store are not always bad. Uncertainty is undesirable for humans, as it makes us feel unsafe and uncomfortable, so we try to plan everything out perfectly. That's one reason that we love to acquire things: It feels like it brings a bit of certainty into our lives. But often, it's the things we can't plan for that turn out to be the best part of our experiences.

Now, this is just one example. And buying a second swimsuit may not be frugal, but it is being resourceful. See how resourceful you can be if there's something you don't have, and how easy it can be to acquire it?

One reason that people don't want to get rid of the things they own is that they worry that they will someday need it, and that day will come, and they won't have it. But with Amazon, Wal-Mart and other huge department stores, you can always get anything you really need, if you really need it. And often, you will find that you don't really need something, but there is a way around it, like borrowing it from a neighbor or friend. (Which is even more money-saving!)

When you pare down, you have to accept that you will sometimes have that feeling of "I wish I hadn't gotten rid of that!" But know that it will be OK. Just like in the vacation example, you will bounce back, find a way, and maybe have more fun being creative. It can be easier and more fun to be resourceful than digging through drawers of things to find that one item. And what's the point of carrying one item from house to house every time you move and finding a place to store it just to use it twice in 20 years?

In the next chapter, we will look at another mindset that may help you get rid of your things.

9 RENTER'S MINDSET

THE RENTER'S MINDSET IS A way to approach all the things that you feel like you "own" in your life. Do you really "own" them? What does "ownership" mean?

"Ownership," in common terms, means that you have exchanged money with a vendor to acquire the item, you got a receipt of the transaction (a legal document proving that you purchased the item), and you keep it in your home or apartment, with all of the other things you own.

But owning something doesn't take away the certainty of it never leaving you. Maybe you will lose an item walking down the street when it falls out of your bag. Maybe a (God-forbid) house fire takes all of your things away from you by destroying them. "Owning" something does not mean that it brings certainty into your life, or that you can truly own it. Unlike the ancient Egyptians, who believed that you need to bring many possessions with you in your coffin to the afterlife, in modern society and many interpretations of the world's great religions, we do not believe that we need to take possessions with us in death, or into an afterlife, whichever you believe.

Not to get too heavy in this book by bringing up death, but I believe it is important to think about your own death when you think about why you are acquiring things. It may be scary, but it is ultimately freeing, and I believe it makes us live more fully in the present moment. In Ancient Rome, great war heroes would have a slave follow them around to whisper "Momento mori." This Latin phrase roughly translates to "Remember that you will die." It was intended to keep the heroes humble after great victory, but we can co-opt this strategy (without slaves) to keep us mindful of our true values in life.

Like we discussed in the chapter about a life of abundance, it is often intangibles, like our relationships, our work and our health, that bring us true and lasting happiness. Someday, you will die. We all will die. And you cannot bring the latest iPhone with you. You cannot bring your favorite DVD from your collection. You cannot bring your fine China dishes you spent days agonizing over when selecting them for your wedding registry. So why worry so much about these things?

Some people might argue that this sort of thinking leads to nihilism, or the belief that nothing matters and life is meaningless. But I see two choices you can make. One, yes, is nihilism. But the other is adopting the Renter's Mindset in life.

So what is the Renter's Mindset? The Renter's Mindset is the opposite of the owner's mindset. The renter recognizes that "ownership" is a false feeling of certainty, and that we are truly renting ever single thing in our lives, including our possessions, our home (even if we "own" it), our relationships, and especially, our time on this Earth. Once you wrap your head around this more philosophical concept, you will be able to approach things with less anxiety and more freedom. You will not need to worry about buying the latest gadget or get wrapped up in "keeping up with the Joneses." You will not feel the superficial pull of these things when you are able to see yourself as just borrowing each of the items you buy. You will not feel afraid of losing the things you acquire (or feel so much pressure to acquire them) when you realize you will have to give them up eventually, no matter what.

The Renter's Mindset is a bit ethereal and philosophical, so do not worry if you don't really get it or don't find it helps you in your minimalism quest. Take and apply what you find helpful from these philosophical chapters, and feel free to discard what you don't. (In true minimalist fashion!)

This chapter concludes our more philosophical discussions of minimalism, and in the rest of the book, we will get to practical applications of minimalism, and how declutter your home, your digital life and your schedule.

10 Decluttering Principles

As we prepare for the decluttering chapters of this book, let's look at a few general principles that we can apply as we go through our things. These general principles will guide you as you make decisions of what to keep and what to get rid of.

If you can decide on some general rules, values and principles before starting decluttering, you will have a handy list of heuristics (rules of thumb) to reference when you are having trouble making a decision.

Here are few decluttering principles you may find helpful when you get stuck:

1. If you haven't used an item in the last 12 months, and you could easily acquire it again for under $20, you should get rid of it. (It will be difficult to put this into practice. Getting rid of something when you think you should keep it "just in case," is hard, but with each thing you release, it will become easier. Remember to have the Renter's Mindset)

2. Did you remember you had this item? If you didn't know you had it, you probably haven't been missing it. This item can be let go of.

3. Have you used this item in the last six months? Outside of season-specific clothes, if you haven't used something in the last six months, you rarely use it, and keeping it around is probably causing more of a drain on your resources (atorage, care, loss of resale value) than it is worth. You can play with this number to see how it suits you.

Maybe you want to do three months. Or one year. Choose what feels best and what helps you make the best decluttering decisions for you.

Those three guiding principles will help you get rid of most of the objects that are cluttering your life needlessly. De-cluttering and minimizing is a process that, if done right, will take a bit of time. While it is not good to sit and agonize over decisions forever, if you declutter too quickly, you will not have gone through the process in an emotional way, and you will probably find yourself filling up your home again with needless items. You have to stay mindful of the big picture, and not each specific item.

So, as you delve into these next four decluttering chapters, keep in mind *why* you are decluttering. That is why the philosophical chapters of this book are so important. Once you start going through your items, the task may feel daunting, impossible, emotionally exhausting, and not worth it.

If you can, write down a short list of what you can gain by decluttering.

For example:

If I declutter the spare bedroom, I can have more friends and family visit, and strengthening those relationships will bring me happiness.

If I declutter the kitchen, I will have more room to cook healthy meals that make me feel good.

If I get rid of half of my wardrobe, I won't have to spend as much time deciding what to wear in the morning, and I can get more sleep.

This list will remind you just why you are taking on this difficult task, and keep you motivated.

Now, onto the decluttering!

11 DECLUTTER YOUR HOME

DECLUTTERING YOUR HOME MAY BE the hardest decluttering task you face, depending on how large your home is and how many things you have acquired over the years. Even if you live in a simple studio apartment, it is worth going through your things.

Your initial declutter will probably take a while, but once you have completed it, you will only need minimal maintenance forever after. Once you are aware of why you are brining so many items into your life, you will stop wanting them and buying them. You may even find you will keep getting rid of more and more things over the years, as you fill your life up with abundance in other ways.

For the first round of decluttering, you don't need to accomplish this all in a weekend, and I advise you don't. You will feel rushed, stressed, emotionally overwhelmed, and probably have a breakdown and want to give up. I suggest focusing on one room each weekend, and taking a month or two to go through all your things. It's not a race to minimalism, remember. Proceed at your own pace, and with what feels right.

If you don't live alone, it should be noted that you will need to bring up the topic of your newfound minimalism with the people you live with. You can't get rid of something someone else owns, or something someone else felt was a commonly-owned item shared by everyone in your living space. How you want to approach this conversation varies, but shouldn't be taken lightly. If you are serious about committing to a fuller, richer and simpler life, you will need to convey your seriousness to your roommates, children, spouse, or whomever you live with. They may judge you or think you are crazy for wanting to get rid of all the wonderful stuff you own. Prepare for this reaction, but know that you are making the right decision for your life. Let them know that you will be going through your own items, but will not disrupt their things. You can explain why you are making the change, and you may find that they become a bit interested in minimalism.

However, many people are not so interested in living a life of minimalism. They may say, "I wish I could do that, but I just need all my things" or "I wish I could do what you do, but I just love shopping too much." People love to make excuses about why they can't change, and you can't force anyone to change. However, you can make steps to make sure they don't prevent you from changing. When I first started practicing minimalism, I knew I'd take a lot of my things to the Goodwill to donate them. I wanted someone else to be able to use the things that I didn't. So, I thought it was kind to offer my friends and family members first-pick to use the items I knew I would be happier without. But this caused me more grief than pleasure. People would not only keep nearly everything I tried to give away, they'd judge me in the process. "Woah, you're just throwing this away?" they'd ask. "How could you get rid of this? I'll keep it for you until you want it back." So beware of letting your friends and family be too involved in the process if they do not have the same mindset as you.

As you go through the rooms of your home, there is a process that I recommend for decluttering. The process can take a bit of time, so make sure you have a few days to really commit to it, otherwise you (or your housemates) may go crazy from all the stuff you've pulled out and left everywhere.

First, you should pull everything in a room out. Yes, everything. Drawers, cabinets, closets, find it all. Then, start going through everything, item by item. You will have three piles into which to put things: Yes/Keep, No/Get Rid Of and Maybe.

Yes/Keep items are things that you immediately know you use. You have used it in the last week for sure, and maybe you use it almost every day. It's something that you find incredibly helpful, and is an item that fits the 20% part of the 80/20 Rule (You get 80% of the use out of 20% of your things.)

No/Get Rid Of items are things you can't remember using, or haven't used in the last six months to a year. They fall in the 80% of the 80/20 rule. (80% of your things you use 20% of the time). Here is where it is easy to fall into the "what-if" and the "just-in-case" trap. You imagine in your head a scenario where you will need the thing in an emergency, if some unusual situation comes up, or if you finally host that dinner party you've talked about hosting but never have for the last 10 years. Well, dear reader and newfound minimalist, it is time: Time to finally let go. Time to finally accept your life. Time to be more free. If you can replace the item fairly easily (at a store within a short drive, or a purchase on Amazon) for less than $20, it should go.

The Maybe items will be the trickiest. They will be the things that you find sentimental value in, that you use sometimes but not very often, or that you're just not sure about. That is OK. Don't let a Maybe item stall you for hours as you contemplate its usefulness. Just recognize a Maybe item when you see it and put it in the Maybe pile. Maybe items will be put in storage, out of sight, so they can not easily be gotten, for three months or six months. If you haven't missed an item, or found it worth it to go digging through packed-away boxes to pull it out, then you can safely get rid of it after the allotted time you have chosen. You won't even need to open the Maybe boxes and go through all the items again, as it will cause you further grief and anguish trying to decide once again if the Maybe items are worth keeping or not. When the three months, or six months, or however long you decide on, is up, just grab the boxes, don't look inside, and drop them off at the Goodwill. Decisions made!

Of course, there will be some exceptions to these rules, and I'll discuss a few special cases and considerations below:

Bedroom

Making your bedroom as comfortable and simple as possible may help you sleep at night. Many people use their bedrooms as a place to work, get distracted by their phone and scroll endlessly for a long time, pay bills, or do a lot of things besides intentional relaxing and sleep. If you make your bedroom a place solely for sleep and pre-sleep relaxation, like reading or your end-of-day gratitude lists, your brain will instantly shift into "sleep mode" when you are in your bedroom. I recommend that you think about making your bedroom a place of rest when you declutter, as sleep is such an important part of a healthy life.

Books

If you are an avid reader (as you probably are if you've picked up this little book), you may have an extensive collection of books that you are proud of. I once owned hundreds of books. The problem was, most of them were unread. They were "someday" books. They were aspirational books. They were the books I'd probably have time to read when I also got that promotion, lost 10 pounds, and had a chic wardrobe. My bookshelf also involved many of my favorites, book that I actually *had* read. But I wasn't pulling them out to read them every day. In fact, I wasn't re-reading them even once a year. That meant my book collection, while it looked nice, wasn't doing a whole lot for my day-to-day-life. It was part of the 80% of my possessions I was using 20% of the time (Or realistically, maybe 1%). I spent a ton of money on books, as I loved browsing bookstores and reading "Best Books" lists, but I never seemed to get around to actually reading them or finishing them.

Now, I've embraced libraries and digital books. While you may have to wait a bit longer to borrow a library book, rather than buying it at a bookstore, it is good exercise in patience, and has significantly cut down my impulse purchases. I now use a Kindle reader to read many books as well, which has cut down my bookshelf space quite a bit. I got rid of all my books, and know that with the internet, anything I need to reference can be found with only a few clicks. Getting rid of books doesn't mean you aren't a reader or a bookworm, if that is a large part of your identity. It just means that you don't need a bookshelf full of books to portray yourself that way to people, and you can still read as much as your heart desires through other means.

Collectibles

Many people are avid collectors. Maybe you collect postcards of your travels, model trains, DVDs of your favorite movies, or rare editions of books. If your collection is very important to you, and it brings joy into your life, then of course, don't get rid of it. Minimalism is about deciding what is important to you, and cutting out what isn't important, and what is just a clutter and distraction. So if you really get joy out of your collection, keep it. However, really think about your collection before automatically deciding to keep it. Another essential aspect of minimalism is investigating the emotional reasons for having things. So as long as you spend some time thinking about it, considering your reasons, and decide it is part of your new abundant but simple life, then you are good.

Garage

Growing up, my family garage was rarely used for an actual car. It was most often used to store a ton of toys, lawn equipment, and miscellaneous junk. I advise trying to use your garage for your car. But it may mean getting rid of a lot of items.

Sentimental Items

Items that hold sentimental value are one of the most difficult categories to work through when decluttering your home. It is easy to keep every birthday greeting card we ever receive, every gift we get, and every receipt from a memorable vacation. But are these things bringing abundance and happiness to your life, or are you only keeping them because you fear getting rid of them? One helpful way to think about your sentimental items is to realize that if you keep everything, then it reduces the value of your sentimental items. However, if you only keep the most sentimental, then you have made those few items very important. If you have 300 school assignments from your grade school days, or those of your children, it can feel very emotional and cruel to get rid of them. But how often do you sit down and go through all 300 of these? If you go through the stack and pick five or 10 that you find very meaningful, you can keep these. Maybe you can even choose just one, and then you can frame it and hang it up in a place of prominence in your home. Then, instead of having 300 pages and projects gathering dust and never appreciated, you have just one item that you can look at and appreciate every day. It doesn't mean you don't care, it just means that you are caring intentionally and in a way that makes sense.

It is the same with greeting cards or gifts. If you have kept every card your aunt has ever sent you, they, too, are probably in a box hiding somewhere. You know what would be more meaningful than keeping all her cards, something neither you, nor her, probably think about on a daily basis, or ever? Call up your aunt and take her to lunch. That hour you spend talking with her is much more aligned with living an abundant life than keeping her cards. The next logical step to consider, however, is the death of a loved one. If your aunt has passed, getting rid of her cards may seem cruel. In this case, I'd recommend the grade school art strategy. Choose something that would make you think of your aunt and how much she meant to you, and display it somewhere. This is more meaningful than keeping an object just because. And remember that what is most important in our lives is the people themselves, and our relationships with those people do not exist in objects. They exist in our experiences, memories and feelings. You have the power to remember them, the power does not lie in physical things.

One way to "keep" sentimental items without having to physically store them is to take digital photos of them, or scan them into your computer. You can keep digital photos, which will be nice reminders if you want to pass them down in your family, but then no one is responsible for keeping boxes and boxes of things.

Seasonal Items

Christmas decorations, other holiday decorations or seasonal wear will be harder to assess than everyday items, as you use them occasionally but maybe have not in the last six months. Some of the regular rules apply, though. Remember that less is more. Do you need all the Christmas decorations you have, or could you pare down to just the things you really love and get joy from? We will discuss clothing in a following chapter.

I hope this list has given you the tools you need to get started on decluttering your home. Do you have a conundrum in your decluttering, or a question about this chapter? As you go through your decluttering journey, if you want to reach out to me about something from this book, I am happy to help. You can reach me at contact@walnutpub.com, and put in the subject "To Aston."

In the next chapter, we will look at decluttering your digital life, another important aspect of all of our lives in this day and age.

12 Declutter Your Devices

In this chapter, we will discuss decluttering your digital life and devices. In this day and age, we all live so much of our lives online. We shop online, we social network online, we send email instead of letters, we work online, we read on a digital device, we listen to music on our phone or computer, we take digital photos that we may never print out. We do everything online, and sometimes it can feel like our digital existence is as cluttered, if not more so, than our physical one.

While all the information from our online lives is digital, and it therefore doesn't take up a lot of space in our physical life, it still weighs on us mentally. It is still clutter that can make us feel anxious, like our minds are constantly racing, and like we have too much to do and too much going on.

So paring down your digital life is also important to living a life of minimalism, and enjoying a life of abundance.

How can you minimize your digital life?

Pare Down Your Apps & Notifications

Looking at a cluttered phone screen sends our mind racing. With so many apps to check, and apps that send us notifications, our attention gets diverted and divided thousands of times throughout the day. Keep only the apps that you find truly essential, that you really need, or that you really get good use out of. It can take just 15 minutes to go through and declutter your phone by erasing old apps you downloaded but never use, get rid of distracting and time-wasting games, and hiding your other time-wasting apps on screens other than your home screen. If you have a bad habit of checking your phone and unlocking it often, but after decluttering you can unlock it to a very simple or blank screen, you will be less likely to check it all the time moving forward. Having a decluttered screen can feel like having a decluttered mind.

Organize Your Files

Decluttering can be the same on your laptop, desktop computer or an external hard drive. Organize your documents so that you know where to find them. You may find that you can delete a lot of old documents as well, or move them all into an "old documents" folder. Once you know that all your old files have been sorted, you will feel fresher.

Check Social Media/Email Less Frequently

It is a bad habit to check your phone all the time, and doing this habit on a daily basis actually rewires your brain for scattered, shallow and distracted thinking. You get better at jumping from task to task, but you sacrifice the ability to concentrate, think deeply, or work hard on something for a sustained period. Breaking this habit is essential to reclaiming your mind, and truly 'decluttering' your brain.

Unsubscribe With Abandon

One tactic that can help with feeling like you are always behind on emails, work and catching up on notifications is unsubscribing from as much as you can. Whenever you sign up for a website, buy something online, or sign up for a service, you get subscribed by email to a newsletter of some kind. These newsletters can quickly get out of control. The best way to keep your email inbox clean is to prevent the emails from coming in in the first place. Unsubscribe from as much as you can. Even if you fear missing out on a piece of news, or one deal, is it really worth it to read that one news article or get 10% off a certain item, if instead you can reclaim all that time you waste opening and discarding the hundreds of emails it takes to find the relevant one? I personally have unsubscribed from so many emails that now, the only emails I receive that are not work-related are personal email from friends and family, and one newsletter from a website I like reading that comes once every two weeks. As soon as I am auto-added to a new email list, I immediately unsubscribe. This strategy has helped erase so much digital clutter in my life, and I can rest easy knowing that my inbox is always clean and only contains emails that are actually relevant to me.

Have Intentional Disconnected Time

Most of us spend 100% of our time "connected." We get email notifications on our phones, check our social media sites every hour (if not every 15 minutes), and are available at any time to receive a phone call or text from someone and respond. But this constant connectedness is having a negative impact on our lives. We sometimes ignore the people we love when we spend time with them by checking our phone. Our brains become easily distracted, and we find it difficult to focus. We crave constant information and distraction.

Practicing intentional time to disconnect from it all will feel incredibly uncomfortable at first. Going for a 15-minute walk without your phone might make you feel naked. What if there is an emergency? What if you get lost and need GPS? What if you get an important email? These irrational fears keep us tethered to our phones. Instead, take a deep breath, and realize that there is nothing so important that it can't wait 15 minutes. Practice going places without your phone, or leaving your phone in another room of the house when you are trying to focus on reading a book or getting a task done. It will take your practice, but over time, you will begin to relish the time you can spend disconnected. You will find you can focus better, you don't constantly crave distraction, and you feel more relaxed.

Overall, doing some digital declutter maintenance will make you feel a bit less scattered. But in addition to organizing our devices and files, it is also a good minimalist habit to not need to feel connected to many social networking sites and email constantly. While these sites can be a good way to share with friends and family and keep in touch, not to mention stay on top of work, they lead to a distracted mind. A decluttered mind is one that can appreciate the here and now, and not get lost in a cycle of instant gratification.

In the next chapter, we will look at decluttering your time and schedule.

13 DECLUTTER YOUR SCHEDULE

SOMETIMES, IT CAN FEEL LIKE there is so much to do. We are busy at work, we are busy in our home lives, we are busy in our free time. It can feel like there is just no time. We want to get to the gym, but there is no time. We want to start a daily writing habit, but there is just no time. We want to spend more time with someone we care about, but we just can't find the time.

Being a minimalist with your time means going back to that tenet of minimalism: Cut out the inessential, to allow the essential to grow abundantly.

What Brings You Satisfaction?

Here, the 80/20 rule comes into play again. What tasks are you spending 80% of your time on, but only getting 20% of the results in your life from? For example, are you doing an easy workout for 90 minutes, when you could be doing a very difficult workout in 30 minutes? Are you splitting your attention between social media, email, and your work tasks? Studies show that multitasking actually leads to completing fewer tasks in a timely manner. You could instead focus on one thing at a time and see much better results. Are there activities you could just eliminate from your life entirely to cut down on wasted time?

For example, what you doing because you feel like you "need" to, or are "supposed to," but you don't actually want to? Do you feel like you should be gardening to keep up with the neighbors, but you don't actually get that much satisfaction from it, and would rather spend your time doing yoga, or re-connecting with friends, or writing, or anything else? You could either hire a gardener, or just let the lawn go natural. You get to decide what is worth your limited time on this Earth to do, and should not feel trapped in what other people think is important.

Keep Track

One tactic to use when you are trying to declutter your schedule is to keep track of what you spend your time on. When people are trying to stick to a diet, they are often told to keep a food diary. It is the same for budgeting and spending. When you have to write down what you eat or spend, you become more aware of it, and have data to see what is really going on.

So keep a log of your time for a week or a month, and it will definitely surprise you. Log every minute, if you can. How long does your morning routine take? How much time do you spend online? How much time watching TV? How much time at the gym? Log everything, and then see where you are "overspending" your time, and what essential activities that you claim are important to you are actually getting the short end of the stick.

Say No

It can be difficult to say "no" to someone. Many of us like to please other people. We like to be helpful, agreeable and nice. Saying "no" without a concrete excuse can feel like being rude and selfish. But learning how to say "no" is freeing. We all have obligations that we feel like we can't change. We have to be in the office for a certain number of hours per week, we have to help that junior coworker who asked for mentorship, we have to attend our friend's barbecue, we have to go the gym seven days a week to maintain our fitness.

With your new minimalist mindset, however, you should question whether these non-negotiables are really that non-negotiable. If you are trying to declutter your time and schedule, look once again at what is bringing you the most satisfaction and happiness, and what you are attending out of feelings of obligation.

Let's look at some examples. For the junior coworker who wants mentorship, you would feel guilty if you said no. But is it really best for her to have a mentor who feels like they have to say yes, versus a mentor who is actually very excited to take her under their wing? For your friend's barbecue, do you feel like you have to attend because you have nothing else going on that day, but you actually aren't excited about it? Do you imagine all the things you could get done if you had that Saturday afternoon free? People often feel like they have to have a reason to say no to something. But you may be surprised how much people respect a firm "no" given without an excuse. If you just say, "I'm sorry, but I won't be able to attend," most polite people won't probe further to ask you why. They will respect your "no."

We often feel in our society that spending time just by ourselves is not a valid excuse to say no. But why shouldn't your priorities and values be the best reason to say no? If you have dedicated Saturday afternoons as the time you take up the guitar and practice, then just because you have scheduled that time by yourself, and are only accountable to yourself, that doesn't mean it's not a great reason to turn down social invitations. Don't be afraid of saying a simple "no." Stand up for yourself and your time. It's the only way to make sure there's enough time in the day for the things that are important to you. Saying "yes" to every opportunity, invitation and request that comes your way is a sure-fire way to stay over-scheduled, stretched thin and stressed.

Now let's look at the other two obligations: Your job and your fitness. For your job, you may be surprised just how negotiable your job is. You feel you have to be at work 40 hours per week, but what if you asked your boss for a work-from-home day once every two weeks? With remote work becoming more and more mainstream, this request may not be as unreasonable as you think. Saving one day of commute, being able to throw a load of laundry in during the day, and being able to be home for a repair or service worker to come by the home will save hours of time in your week. You may have to start small, and prove to your boss you are actually working just as hard at home by doing a few trial afternoons, but don't think that working from home is too extreme of an idea.

Minimalism is about questioning the status-quo, when it comes to our objects and our time. Women are stereotypically supposed to have at least a dozen pairs of shoes, but why? You have to investigate these beliefs that you may not have questioned before, just like the belief that it is necessary for you to be in your office to get work done.

As for fitness, maintaining a healthy lifestyle is important. But when it comes to trimming your obligations and freeing up more time, ask yourself, "Am I working harder, or smarter?" Getting to the gym seven days a week is admirable, but could you be cutting out one or two workouts a week, and letting your muscles relax with rest days? Could you change your workout style to do more impactful exercises just three or four days a week? Can you listen to an audiobook during your workout, and therefore read and exercise at the same time? Try to question the things you see as set in stone, and you may find that you can free up so much more time in your day that you thought possible.

In minimalism, managing your time and energy is as important as managing your stuff. In the next chapter, we will look at decluttering your closet.

14 Capsule Wardrobe

The 80/20 rule especially applies to our wardrobe. You have your favorite outfits, shirts, accessories and items. Imagine these items in your mind. When you wear them, you probably feel the most "you." They fit your personality, and your style. They make you feel good about your body and the way you look. You probably wear these clothes 80% of the time. Most of your clothes just sit in your closet, and you only wear them occasionally. Maybe they don't fit quite right, or the color, in retrospect, doesn't look that great on you. Maybe you can't quite place your finger on why you don't enjoy wearing that clothing, but for some reason, it sits unworn in your closet most of the time. It is part of the 80% of your clothes that you wear 20% of the time.

The capsule wardrobe is the idea of a style of dress that comes from French origins. The idea is to have classic and basic clothing items that you love, and that can all be mixed and matched with each other. With just a total of 30 items, you create dozens if not hundreds of different looks, once you add in different shoes and accessories.

Now, the capsule wardrobe might not be for you. Maybe you love bright colors or flashy patterns, and having just a few items that all go together wouldn't work with your personal style. That's OK, the idea of a capsule wardrobe is to realize the things that you wear most, and treat those items with care.

Another thing to think about when it comes to clothes is investing in quality. "Fast fashion" stores like H&M and Forever 21 produce extremely cheap clothes that are highly fashionable. But they tend to wear down very quickly, and you have to keep buying new clothes.

However, if you purchase high-quality, classic clothing items, you can keep these clothing items around for years if you take care of them.

Most people won't notice if you simplify your wardrobe. People are too self-focused to notice that you have a minimal, classic style that you recycle often. In fact, you will look very well put-together all the time. Wouldn't it be great to feel stylish, the most "you," and comfortable all of the time, instead of feeling like you need to wear your clothes you don't really like sometimes, just because they're there?

Simplifying your wardrobe means that you will have fewer decisions to make in the course of the day, especially when you first wake up and need your brain power to focus on more important tasks. You will find that you save so much time and stress over what to wear, and instead, you will be able to divert that time and attention on to more meaningful parts of your life, just like when you pare down your possessions, your schedule, and your devices.

I recommend decluttering your closet in the same fashion as you decluttered the rest of your house. Those tips can be found in the "Declutter Your Home" chapter. Go once again through making Keep, Discard and Maybe piles, and keep the Maybe items hidden for a certain amount of time. Following those steps, you can free up your closet space and trim your wardrobe.

In the next and final chapter, we will discuss a closing though on minimalism and essentialism.

15 Conclusion: Essentialism

THANK YOU FOR READING THIS guide to minimalism. We covered a lot of ground about this philosophy of life, including emotional questioning, practical tips for decluttering, and what it all means and what it's all for. What I hope you take away from this book is that minimalism doesn't need to mean getting rid of as much stuff as you can. It is all about essentialism. Get rid of what is inessential to become abundant in what is essential.

Minimalism is tailor-made for me, for you, and for everyone. Choose how much of it you want to adopt in your life. If you want to have a huge wardrobe, and you genuinely get joy out of wearing each piece of clothing you have, then own as many clothes as you like. If you love your Trolls collection with all your heart, then keep them. Don't let anyone else judge your possessions or tell you what should matter to you.

However, that doesn't mean minimalism is simple. Making the distinction between the essential and the inessential can be difficult. The lines are often gray, not black and white, and it's hard to figure out what feels good right now versus what feels good in a healthy, real and sustaining way over a lifetime. Choosing a life of minimalism means really investigating what you have that makes you happy, and what is extra, wasteful and a drag on your time, resources and energy. Cut out all that extra stuff without mercy and focus on only what will truly matter, in the end, to you.

Our time on this Earth is limited. Our brain chemistry seeks out what is instant, flashy and seductive. Often, that means shopping and purchasing and hoarding things we don't need. It means apps that notify us and ping us for interaction as often as possible for little tangible reward. It means overbooked schedules so that we never have to miss out, say "no," or really invest deeply. But minimalism is here to liberate you from all that noise. You don't need all that. You're better than that. I'm better than that. And we all deserve better than that.

I hope that your journey with minimalism has begun here, but that it leads to a lifelong journey of noticing your life, living with intentionality, experiencing life more deeply, and choosing what you spend your time and money on, instead of letting your impulses choose for you. I sincerely believe you can choose to be happier with a life of minimalism.

I sincerely hope that you begin to lead a life of abundance once you adopt some or all of the principles of minimalism. It may not be easy at first, but it is worth all the hard work you will put in, I can guarantee that.

Thanks for reading.

16 Epilogue: Interview with the Author

BELOW, FIND AN INTERVIEW WITH author Aston Sanderson about his own journey to minimalism.

How did you minimalism journey start?

Like the example I use in this book, I first thought about minimalism when I lost some luggage during a week-long vacation. I was devastated, because I really carefully considered how I would pack for the trip. But after two days, I let go that my stuff wasn't coming (It was actually being held for me back at my home airport, it somehow never made it on the plane). And I just felt so free, it was like nothing I had experienced before. It was fun to just buy things as I needed them. First, a new t-shirt and pair of shorts, then a toothbrush, then a book, and that was basically all I needed. I felt so relaxed on that trip like I hadn't before on a vacation. So I started thinking about what it would be like to kind of live your life that way, just acquiring things as you needed them, and not worrying if they disappeared one day.

Where do the ideas in this book come from?

I started experimenting with minimalism before I ever knew there was this whole movement that had a name. I just called it "lost luggage life" in my head, or when I tried to describe it to friends. When I got back from that trip, I packed all my things away, and then would just take out what I used as I used it. I'd say about 80% of my stuff I never unpacked, just like the Pareto principle I talked about in this book. So most of the book comes from personal experience, but I've also read a lot of Buddhist and Stoic philosophy, and I think those ideas come through. The book can feel a bit broad in scope, asking people to look at their life values, but I think it's essential for any meaningful change in your life. As I discovered in my personal minimalism journey, it's not really about the stuff, it ends up being about you and your emotions.

What have been your challenges with minimalism?

I still fall into consumerism patterns now and again. People might think that someone who has written a book on minimalism never has a slip-up, but I still fall into the advertising traps, or consumerism culture, or just thinking that my life will be better with another object in it. I recently bought a new laptop, but if I'm being honest with myself, I didn't really need to. My old one worked fine, I just convinced myself I needed the new one. So, it is hard to keep your life simple, and it's an on-going process.

What's surprised you most during your minimalist journey?

The most surprising thing has been how much time I have when I decluttered my digital life. I was probably checking my email at least 15-20 times a day before, and each time I checked it, either there was new mail that sent me down a rabbit hole of reading or responding or looking at the internet, or there wasn't a new mail, but I fell into an internet time-suck anyway. Now, I check my email once per day, and that's it. I felt before like I had no time in the day to get done what I wanted to, but now that I'm not losing those hours to the internet, I find I have a lot of time on my hands. It's a really good feeling.

How do you friends and family react to your minimalist life?

One of my good friends jokes sometimes how much he "loves things." And he'll say, "Aston, you only own three things." We can joke around and laugh about it, because we're both happy in the way we live our lives, and I'm happy that he is living his life how he wants. I'm not looking to change people that don't want to be change, but just give the people who are unhappy and do want to change the ability and courage to do so. There are a lot of different ways out there to live your life, and I want people to find the one that works best for them. For some people, that may mean my way. For a lot of people, it's probably not my way, and that's OK too. That doesn't mean they are bad people or I don't want to have relationships with them. Most people in my life are not minimalists. It doesn't affect our relationship, unless they try to tell me I need more things, because then they are telling me how to live my life.

My friends and family know not to buy me gifts, though. It can be funny when a new friend tries to grow our relationship by buying my a Christmas present. It's the thought that counts, so it's nice, but my friends will say, "Wow, they must not know you very well at all." Stopping the whole gift-giving thing has been a lifesaver. I save so much money per year not buying gifts for every holiday, birthday, shower and party, and in return, I don't receive a lot of things I don't want from people. Of course, you have to explain to people why you'd like to opt-out of gift-giving. You can't just decide to do it one day and not tell anyone until you don't buy them a gift. But you'd be surprised how many people are relieved that they can remove one gift-giving relationship from their life. By the time you have grand-kids and a huge social network, not to mention coworkers, you just have so many meaningless gifts to buy, it's ridiculous.

I make sure people know I want to spend time with them, not give them gifts. Maybe that means taking someone out for lunch. I think experiences, like paying for a meal, or a day trip, or concert, can be a good alternative to physical gifts.

What do you want readers to take away most from this book?

If readers only took away one thing, I hope it's that minimalism is freeing. If you look at minimalism as just another rigid diet that you have to stick to, it will never work. You really have to look at things with a fresh perspective, and I hope that brings people the freedom in their lives to do what they really love.

Your Feedback is Important to Me

Dear Reader,

Thank you for taking the time to read this book. I hope you got a lot out of it and learned something you can apply to your own life.

If you have any feedback, positive or negative, I'd love to hear from you. I personally read all the reviews on my Amazon page, and hope you'll take a minute to tell me (and other readers) what you think.

Type this URL into your browser to go straight to the review page for this book: bit.ly/minimalistreview

Thank you!

—Aston Sanderson

FURTHER READING

Like what you read?

More Books From This Author

"Self Talk: How to Train Your Brain to Turn Negative Thinking into Positive Thinking & Practice Self Love"

Have racing thoughts, a lot of negative self-talk, or worry and stress a lot? Learn strategies to change the way your thought patterns run and get your inner monologue to work *for* instead of against you. Buy the book at

bitly.com/selftalkbook

"Small Talk: How to Talk to People, Improve Your Charisma, Social Skills, Conversation Starters & Lessen Social Anxiety."

Want to learn how to meet people easily, be free from social anxiety, and be the type of person people love talking to? Buy "Small Talk," now with expanded content to include small talk for dating. By it at

bitly.com/smalltalkbook

"The Stress-Free Baby Names Book: How to Choose the Perfect Baby Name with Confidence, Clarity and Calm"

bitly.com/babynamesbook

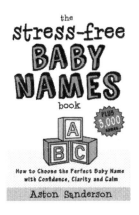

Made in the USA
Columbia, SC
29 October 2020